Contents

Brave and adventurous

I ... hoisted English Colours, and in the Name of His Majesty ... took possession of the whole Eastern Coast ... by the Name of New South Wales ...

James Cook, 22 August 1770

The 17th and 18th centuries were a time of great exploration. Brave adventurers from Europe set out on long and dangerous **voyages**. Many times, they did not have maps to guide them and had very little idea what was waiting for them on the other side of the world.

Mostly the explorers were looking for places that were 'unknown'. They were often sent by the governments of their countries to find more land and useful resources like metals and spices, or trade passages. Other times, explorers were sent to claim and control those parts of the 'new' world that were considered to be valuable. Unfortunately, these explorers often did not recognise the rights of the indigenous peoples who already lived there. The results for these peoples were often tragic.

European explorers gradually mapped the entire world and made contact with people from different cultures. Because of them, the world changed forever.

Did you know?
In the sixth century BCE, the Greek mathematician Pythagoras spoke about a great southern continent that would balance the land in the north.

voyages long journeys, especially by sea

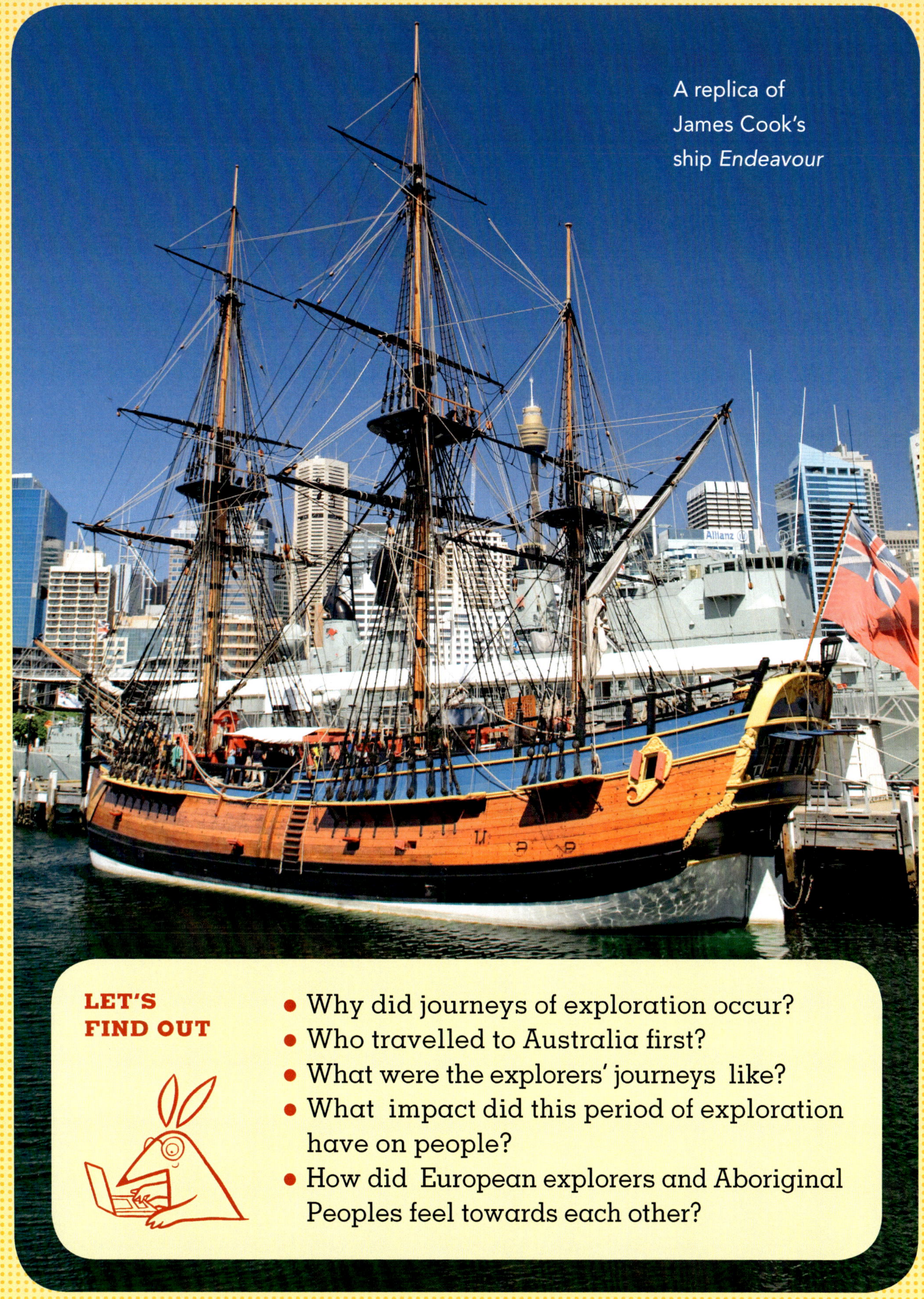

A replica of James Cook's ship *Endeavour*

LET'S FIND OUT

- Why did journeys of exploration occur?
- Who travelled to Australia first?
- What were the explorers' journeys like?
- What impact did this period of exploration have on people?
- How did European explorers and Aboriginal Peoples feel towards each other?

Mapping Australia

Today, the entire world has been explored and mapped, but that hasn't always been the case. European explorers only began to travel to Australia and map the continent in the 1600s.

Ortelius's 1570 world map

Name Abraham Ortelius
Nationality Flemish (from modern-day Belgium)
Ship None
Date 1570
Achievements

- Published a map of the world, in which he guessed a land that looked like Australia and Antarctica

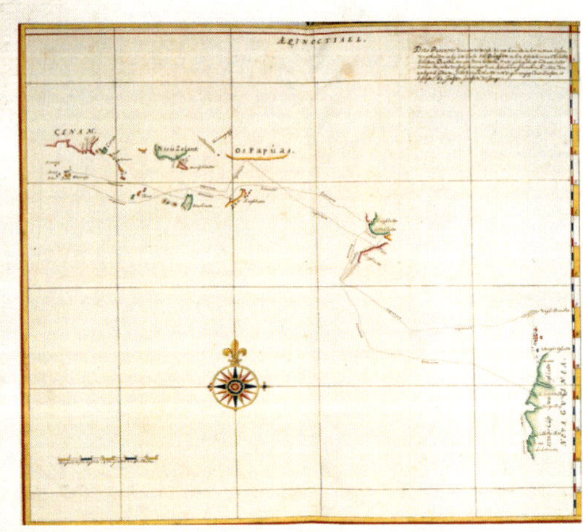

A 1670 copy of the map Janszoon made in 1606

Name Willem Janszoon
Nationality Dutch (from the Netherlands)
Ship *Duyfken*
Date 1606
Achievements

- Became the first European to reach Australia
- Mapped part of Cape York Peninsula, Queensland

continent a great landmass

Dutch map of Australia, 1600s

Name Abel Tasman
Nationality Dutch
Ships *Heemskerk* and *Zeehaan*
Date 1642
Achievements
- Claimed Tasmania and Western Australia for the Netherlands
- Mapped northern Australia

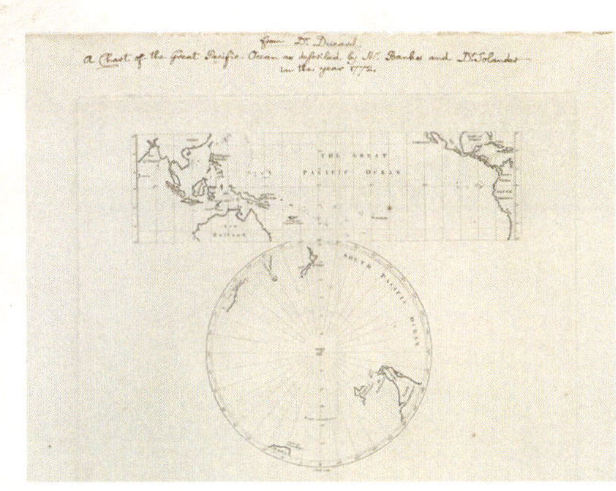
Australia's eastern coast, 1772

Name James Cook
Nationality English
Ship *Endeavour*
Date 1770
Achievements
- Claimed the east of Australia for Britain and named it New South Wales

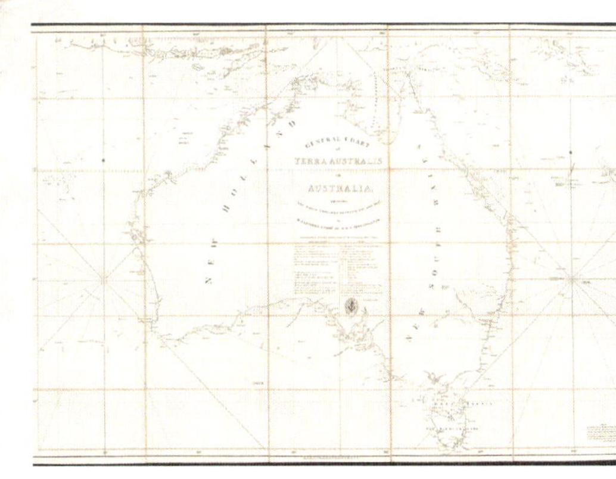
Flinders' 1814 map of Australia

Name Matthew Flinders
Nationality English
Ship *Investigator*
Date 1801–1803
Achievements
- Became the first person to **circumnavigate** Australia
- Produced the first complete map of Australia

circumnavigate to sail all the way around something

Breakaway tasks

Remembering

1 List four explorers who travelled to Australia between the 1600s and 1800s.

2 Make a time line of significant dates from the information in the fact file.

Understanding

3 In 1856, Van Diemen's Land was renamed Tasmania. Which explorer do you think it was named after? Why?

4 Draw a map of Australia, highlighting all of the places mentioned in the fact file. Include their original and current names.

5 Make a multiple-choice quiz about early Australian explorers and map-makers.

Applying

6 Research one of the explorers mentioned in the text. Write a report about him.

Analysing

7 Explain why you think much of Earth was not mapped until about 600 years ago.

8 Create a checklist of features explorers would have considered before claiming a land.

Evaluating

9 Was it right for explorers to claim parts of Australia? List arguments for and against their actions.

Creating

10 Imagine you have discovered a new island. Name your island and draw a map of it, showing features such as mountains and lakes.

Young Nick's journal

Nicholas Young sailed on the *HMS Endeavour* with Captain James Cook. He was the 'loblolly boy', which means that he was the **surgeon**'s assistant. Nick didn't keep a journal, but let's imagine what he might have written if he did …

26 August 1768, Portsmouth
Today we set sail for Tahiti!

Dr Monkhouse explained my duties. I am to manage the medical supplies and look after sick crew members. I will also help him with surgeries.

I know I'm only a loblolly boy now, but one day I will be a great explorer. I want to discover new lands and have places named after me!

16 January 1769
For two days now, we have battled strong winds and enormous waves. Finally, today we passed **Cape** Horn! Captain Cook says that I'm a real sailor now! I can wear a gold earring to show that I've sailed round 'the horn'.

surgeon doctor
Cape land that sticks out from the mainland

13 July 1769, Tahiti
We left Tahiti today, heading southward. Now we are looking for *Terra Australis*.

6 October 1769
I saw a number of sea birds and seals today. We might see land soon! Here is a picture of the wildlife.

7 October 1769
What a wonderful day! I was in the **crow's nest** when I saw something on the **horizon**. As soon as I realised they were cliffs, I gave the alarm: "Land ahoy!"

The captain clapped me on the back and cried, "Well done, young Nick!" He told me that this was probably the land known as *Nova Zeelandia*. Then the best thing of all happened: he named the headland Young Nick's Head after me!

crow's nest a place high up on a ship for people to look out from
horizon where the land or sea appears to meet the sky

Breakaway tasks

Remembering

1 Describe the job of a loblolly boy.

2 Name two places that Nick travelled to on his journey.

Understanding

3 Draw a comic strip outlining the main events in Nick's journal.

4 What clues in the text suggest that Nick felt hopeful?

Applying

5 Locate Cape Horn on a map of the world. Research why this was a major milestone for sailing ships.

6 Write a journal entry about a trip or journey of your own.

Analysing

7 How was Nick brave and adventurous? Write a script for a television advertisement persuading people to join an expedition.

8 Write a speech, from Captain Cook's point of view, congratulating Nick on his discovery.

Evaluating

9 In your opinion, who plays the more important role on a ship: the captain or the surgeon? Give three reasons for your answer.

Creating

10 Compose a song about Nick's journey on the *Endeavour*. You might like to use the melody of a well-known tune.

Bennelong: Peacemaker and explorer

Woollarawarre Bennelong was born in about 1764. He was a member of the Wangal, who were part of the Eora language group. They were the original **inhabitants** of the Sydney area.

In November 1789, Bennelong and his friend Colebee were kidnapped by British soldiers. They were then taken to the British **settlement** at Sydney Cove. The governor of the settlement, Arthur Phillip, had ordered the kidnapping. The plan was to teach the men to speak English, so they could **interpret** between the British and Aboriginal people.

Portrait of Bennelong, painted by a Port Jackson artist in about 1790

Colebee soon escaped, but Bennelong remained in the settlement for about six months before escaping.

A few months later, Bennelong arranged for Governor Phillip to visit the Eora people. Someone threw a spear at Phillip, injuring his arm. Bennelong stepped in and convinced the governor not to **retaliate**, and the meeting ended peacefully.

inhabitants people living in a place
settlement a place set up for people to live permanently
interpret translate from one language to another
retaliate to react to an attack with another attack

Surprisingly, Bennelong and Governor Phillip became good friends. Bennelong even called Phillip *beanga*, meaning 'father'! And Phillip called Bennelong *doorow*, meaning 'son'.

Bennelong learnt to speak English, and he taught the British about the language and **customs** of his own people. In 1790, Governor Phillip built a hut for Bennelong. Today, the Sydney Opera House stands where Bennelong's hut once stood.

In 1792, Bennelong and another man called Yemmerrawannie embarked on a great voyage to England. They were the very first Aboriginal people to visit Europe!

Portrait of Bennelong in European dress

Bennelong and Yemmerrawannie spent five months on a cramped, uncomfortable ship. When they arrived, the busy streets of London must have seemed strange and even frightening to them. They visited several major tourist sites in London, including the Tower of London and St Paul's Cathedral. They even went to the theatre. They spoke English, dressed as Englishmen and lived as their English **hosts** did.

customs a group of people's usual ways of doing things
hosts people who look after visitors

After about a year, Yemmerrawannie became ill and died. Bennelong was terribly upset, and became very homesick. In February 1795, he set sail for Sydney. He arrived in September 1795 – almost three years after he had left. He continued his work with the British for a few years, and made many lifelong friends among the settlers. He died in 1813.

Bennelong played an important role in the development of the British settlement at Sydney Cove. His influence can be seen in a number of place names, including the federal **electorate** of Bennelong.

Bennelong left the country, people and traditions of his homeland and travelled to the other side of the world. He did not captain great voyages, or discover new lands, but he was willing to learn about peoples and cultures that were very different from his own. Bennelong was a true explorer, with a brave and adventurous spirit.

Bennelong Point, Sydney (named after Bennelong)

electorate an area represented by one member of parliament in the government

Breakaway tasks

Remembering

1 Who were the original inhabitants of the area around Sydney?

2 Name two people, other than Bennelong, mentioned in the text. Explain who they are.

Understanding

3 Make a glossary of 10 words from the text.

4 Complete a PMI chart about Governor Arthur Phillip's 'kidnapping' plan. Consider the pluses, minuses and interesting points about this plan.

Applying

5 Draw a time line of key events from Bennelong's life.

6 Research one of the people mentioned in the text, other than Bennelong, and write a biography of that person.

Analysing

7 In the text, we are told that Bennelong and Governor Phillip became good friends. Find two pieces of evidence from the text that support this claim.

8 Why do you think Bennelong chose to leave the British settlement and return to his people?

Evaluating

9 Give three reasons why the British would have found it important to have Aboriginal interpreters.

Creating

10 Imagine you are Bennelong and write a series of personal journal entries about your trip to England.

First impressions

It is 1808. Grace and her friend Hannah have travelled from England to New South Wales on board the ship *Indispensable*. Together, they embark on the adventure of a lifetime, as they start a new life in a new land. In this extract, we see their new home through Grace's eyes.

***Our Australian Girl: Meet Grace*, by Sophie Laguna**

Grace looked at the new land she was approaching. Sydney Cove was **edged** with grey-green trees. They were different to the trees in England. Their silver-green leaves were long and narrow and their trunks were the colour of smoke, but they were definitely the right way up. Flocks of strange white birds flew through the sky, their heads crowned in **tufts** of yellow.

As they rowed closer to land, Grace saw white cottages with red roofs lining dusty criss-crossing roads and men working everywhere … Grace looked out for the giant rats Anne May had told them about, but she didn't see any.

"It really is the other end of the world," Hannah whispered.

Source: *Our Australian Girl: Meet Grace*, by Sophie Laguna, Puffin Books, Penguin Australia, 2011

edged bordered
tufts a bunch of things, e.g. feathers, joined at the base

Breakaway tasks

Remembering

1 What was the name of the new land that Grace was approaching?

2 Describe the trees in Grace's new home.

Understanding

3 Draw a picture of Sydney Cove in Grace's time.

4 Grace looked for the 'giant rats' that she had been told about. What type of animal do you think they really were?

5 Think about a time when you went to a new place. How did you feel? Draw a Venn diagram comparing your experiences with Grace's.

Applying

6 Research convicts' conditions in New South Wales and create a mind-map about them.

Analysing

7 Grace was surprised that the trees in Sydney Cove were 'the right way up'. Why do you think she was surprised?

8 Hannah said that Sydney Cove 'really is the other end of the world'. What do you think she meant by this?

Evaluating

9 Make a list of six descriptive words or phrases in the text. Rank them from most interesting to least interesting.

Creating

10 Imagine you are Grace. Write this story as a diary entry. Predict what you think might happen next.

Strands in action

Core tasks

1. Prepare a presentation about an explorer from the 1600s–1800s. Include a profile and a map.
2. Imagine that you are the first human being to travel to a new planet. Write an account of your experiences. Include details of how you travelled there, information about the resources on the planet, details about the inhabitants already living there and a detailed map of the planet.

Extra tasks

1. Make a word web of interesting adjectives that could be used to describe explorers or navigators.
2. Write a cinquain poem about explorers or their discoveries.
3. Create a mind-map about the positive effects the 'Age of Exploration' had on societies. What were the benefits? Use words, images and facts to complete your mind-map.
4. Survey your classmates to find out which countries they, or their ancestors, came from originally. Present the results in a graph. Find out two facts about each country and then share them with your class.

Make your writing more interesting by including similes. Similes use the words 'like' or 'as' to compare two items and create a clearer picture for the reader. For example, 'as bright as a sunflower'.